D0776769

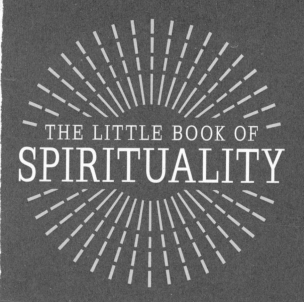

THE LITTLE BOOK OF
SPIRITUALITY

GUIDANCE FOR
A BETTER LIFE

GILLY PICKUP

summersdale

THE LITTLE BOOK OF SPIRITUALITY

Copyright © Summersdale Publishers Ltd, 2015

Written by Gilly Pickup

Summersdale Publishers Ltd
46 West Street
Chichester
West Sussex
PO19 1RP
UK

www.summersdale.com

Printed and bound in the Czech Republic

ISBN: 978-1-84953-713-1

Substantial discounts on bulk quantities of Summersdale books are available to corporations, professional associations and other organisations. For details contact Nicky Douglas by telephone: +44 (0) 1243 756902, fax: +44 (0) 1243 786300 or email: nicky@summersdale.com.

INTRODUCTION

When we begin to explore spirituality, we start our own individual journey to connect with the divine and prevailing force present in our universe. Spirituality, a less prescriptive concept than religion, brings higher levels of serenity, self-acceptance and harmony to your life. As a spiritual being, you will no longer regard challenges as obstacles and you will come to understand that all the answers you seek are already within you. A spiritual life leads to peace and inner calm, contributing greatly to happiness and peace of mind.

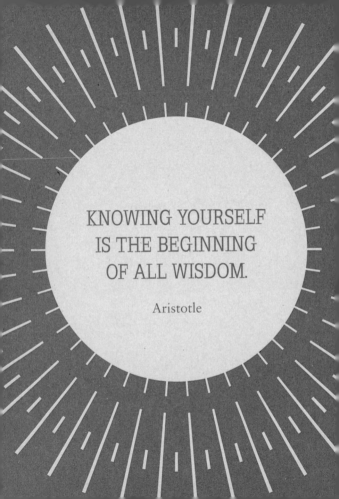

KNOWING YOURSELF
IS THE BEGINNING
OF ALL WISDOM.

Aristotle

Every one of us is a unique being with a distinctive path in life, but it is only when we realise and accept that fact that we are able to open the door to change.

When we grow spiritually, it means we have an awakening and become aware of our inner self. That is when we begin to understand who we really are.

I THINK A SPIRITUAL
JOURNEY IS… A JOURNEY
OF UNCOVERING YOUR
OWN INNER NATURE.
IT'S ALREADY THERE.

Billy Corgan

MINDFULNESS

Mindfulness is the ability to focus on the emotions, thoughts and sensations occurring in the present moment. It can ease a variety of mental conditions, including feeling bored, anxious or worried about a task. Mindfulness teaches us to make a conscious effort to stay in control and focus on the here and now. It teaches us to stop and concentrate on our breathing for a few minutes before continuing, paying close attention to the task in hand. It means our minds aren't flitting from one subject to the next while we are doing one particular thing.

In days gone by, spirituality was connected to organised religion, but as time has passed the meaning of spirituality has changed. For many people nowadays, it is less about religion and more about personal development.

When you follow your spiritual path, try to tap into a feeling of unconditional love. Change negative aspects into positive ones, even when you need to summon up inner strength to do this.

CONCERN FOR OTHERS
IS NOT JUST A MATTER
OF RELIGIOUS PRACTICE;
IT'S A PRACTICAL STEP
TOWARDS CREATING
A HAPPY SOCIETY.

Dalai Lama

FRIENDSHIP HAS ALWAYS
BELONGED TO THE CORE OF
MY SPIRITUAL JOURNEY.

Henri Nouwen

Surround yourself with people who motivate and encourage you and who make you feel good about yourself.

MEDITATION

The word 'meditation' is derived from the Latin *meditari* (to think, dwell on, exercise the mind) and *mederi* (to heal). Its Sanskrit derivation, *medha*, means wisdom. The practice involves finding a quiet place to sit and freeing the mind of scattered thoughts. Try spending 10 minutes simply focusing on your breathing. If your mind wanders, gently draw it back to the gentle action of your breath to create an oasis of calm in your world. This quiet time will help you free yourself to find insights that are lost in the chatter of everyday life.

Pray more or meditate, either in a group or alone, and try to cultivate inner silence. Every time you do this it helps put your spirituality into practice.

There may be challenges to overcome as you begin to live spiritually. You may feel confused as you question beliefs, although the insights you gain can be extremely effective in helping you on your journey. For example, you may be inspired to re-evaluate a bad relationship, or to take on board constructive criticism. As your sense of spirituality grows, it will be easier to face these obstacles and so find inner peace.

YOU HAVE TO GROW
FROM THE INSIDE OUT.
NONE CAN TEACH YOU,
NONE CAN MAKE YOU
SPIRITUAL. THERE IS
NO OTHER TEACHER
BUT YOUR OWN SOUL.

Swami Vivekananda

CHANTING

Chanting consists of the rhythmic speaking of words or sounds and, depending on the culture, can range from simple melodies to complex musical structures. The goal of chanting, or reciting mantras, is to attain a higher state of consciousness and connect with the spiritual. It helps us to develop positive thoughts and is a powerful preparation for meditation.

Create your own happiness mantra: stand in front of a mirror and repeat a positive statement about yourself, in the present tense. Try to do this every day for 3 weeks and you will find that you start to feel better about yourself.

Bring joy into your life. Dance, sing and laugh as often as you possibly can. Remember what it was like to be a child, when unselfconsciousness and spontaneity ruled. Sometimes, as adults, we are afraid to show or feel happiness. Aspire to change that feeling.

MUSIC IS VERY SPIRITUAL;
IT HAS THE POWER TO
BRING PEOPLE TOGETHER.

Edgar Winter

THERE'S NO PAST
AND THERE'S NO
FUTURE. ALL THERE IS,
EVER, IS THE NOW.

George Harrison

Spend 15 minutes a day connecting with yourself. If you choose to do this by meditating, aim to make it the same time every day. Doing this will change your brainwaves and put you into a peaceful state of mind. The effects will last throughout the day.

YOGA

Yoga is a Sanskrit word meaning 'to join or unite'. It generally refers to the union between soul and body and is a practice that supports any religion or belief system. Yoga's poses are aimed at purifying and harmonising the body by using various breathing techniques. There are six limbs of yoga: hatha yoga (which focuses on physical postures), rāja yoga (in which the focus is self-control), bhakti yoga (focusing on devotion), karma yoga (focusing on selfless service), jñāna yoga (to focus the mind) and tantra yoga (focusing on rituals).

Think about things you really enjoy doing – things that make you feel fulfilled. Perhaps it is reading a book by a particular author, walking through the park, meditating, practising Pilates or yoga, or going for a run along the beach. Plan to do something that fulfils you regularly.

Talking or thinking about spirituality might not be something many of us do regularly, and might even feel uncomfortable. However, we should not let that put us off trying to connect with something fundamental and universal that is within all of us.

THE MOST BEAUTIFUL
EMOTION WE CAN
EXPERIENCE IS THE
MYSTICAL. IT IS THE
POWER OF ALL TRUE
ART AND SCIENCE.

Albert Einstein

FOR ATTRACTIVE LIPS,
SPEAK WORDS OF
KINDNESS. FOR LOVELY
EYES, SEEK OUT THE
GOOD IN PEOPLE.

Sam Levenson

One way to grow your spirituality is by helping others. You could, for example, donate to or volunteer for a charity you believe is worthwhile. Whether by giving some money or your time, be more generous in your actions. Learn to give selflessly.

YOGIC BREATHING

Yogic breathing, or *prāṇāyāma*,
helps strengthen the body and
calm and steady the mind.
Defined as the control of life force,
yogic breathing is aimed at increasing
vital energy in the body. The benefits
of this practice are many, including
improved digestion, better focus, an
increased feeling of being centred
and calm, and deeper sleep.

HUMILITY IS NOT
COWARDICE. MEEKNESS IS
NOT WEAKNESS. HUMILITY
AND MEEKNESS ARE INDEED
SPIRITUAL POWERS.

Sivānanda Saraswati

YOU HAVE NOT LIVED A PERFECT DAY… UNLESS YOU HAVE DONE SOMETHING FOR SOMEONE WHO WILL NEVER BE ABLE TO REPAY YOU.

Ruth Smeltzer

Every time you send out a thought, try to make it a positive one. Positive thoughts sweep over everything to reach their objective.

Spiritual wisdom isn't necessarily about mysticism and it does not have to be a part of an organised religion. Reflect on what spirituality means to you and what role you want it to play in your life.

THERE IS MEANING IN
ALL THINGS. BUT ARE YOU
PAYING ATTENTION?

Yasmin Mogahed

LU JONG

This is a form of yoga originally practised in Tibet by Buddhists. Practitioners believe that by following the prescribed movement and breathing exercises they will reach a higher mental state. They also believe that these exercises have medical benefits, which is down to the fact that the practice helps to open all of the chakras (energy centres). Exercises are gentle so that almost anyone can participate.

At the heart of spirituality is peace. If you haven't already found a place of personal sanctuary – anything from a simple garden shed to a tranquil spot high upon a hill – take time to seek one out. Without distractions you will be able to better observe the climate of your inner environment.

Spirituality can provide us with meaning, a sense of strength, the knowledge that we are connected to others. It lets us know that there is 'something bigger' beyond our daily lives. People who feel their life has meaning are generally healthier and happier, too.

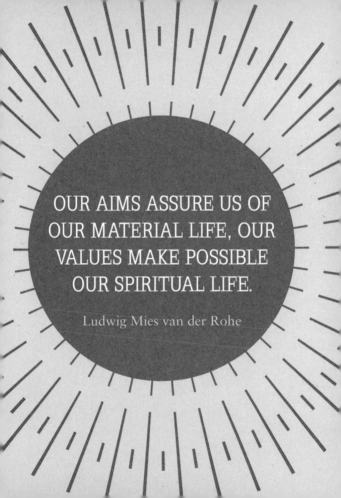

OUR AIMS ASSURE US OF OUR MATERIAL LIFE, OUR VALUES MAKE POSSIBLE OUR SPIRITUAL LIFE.

Ludwig Mies van der Rohe

ULTIMATELY, SPIRITUAL
AWARENESS UNFOLDS
WHEN YOU'RE FLEXIBLE,
WHEN YOU'RE SPONTANEOUS...
WHEN YOU'RE EASY ON
YOURSELF AND EASY
ON OTHERS.

Deepak Chopra

A sense of wonder comes from our natural curiosity about life's journey. Many things awaken our imagination, from the stars in the sky, raindrops, the scent of a rose in the spring or crunching through fallen leaves in autumn. Try to be aware of the amazing, yet everyday, things that are all around us.

Celebrate your senses – smell, touch, sight, hearing, taste – instead of taking them for granted. Be calm, relax and tune into the many ways in which you experience the world.

QIGONG

The word 'qigong' itself translates as 'life energy cultivation' and thus this ancient Chinese practice, a mind–body exercise, cultivates and balances *qi* (chi) or 'intrinsic life energy'. Qigong is designed to raise self-awareness and balance energy by exploring the connection between body, mind and spirit. The co-ordination of body movement, breathing and the resulting mental state assists in maintaining a healthy body and mind. Over time, and with practice, qigong develops mental clarity, so helping to rid practitioners of stress and negative thoughts.

Be at one with nature, whether it is walking in the countryside, along a sandy beach or sitting in a garden or a park. Pay attention to what is around you. Use your senses and ask yourself, 'What do I hear? What can I smell? What do I see?' Concentrating on the here and now can free us from concerns about the past and future, so bringing a sense of calm to our lives.

YOU ARE CREATING YOUR
NEXT MOMENT BASED
ON WHAT YOU ARE
FEELING AND THINKING.
THAT IS WHAT'S REAL.

Doc Childre

Bring happiness into your life by letting go of your regrets. Learn from past mistakes and simply concentrate on the here and now.

Life, for many of us, is frenetic these days. Bring more spiritual feeling into your life by making time, slowing down and listening for guidance from the universe. Simply be open to resources and inner qualities which help us grow.

T'AI CHI

Also called t'ai chi ch'uan, t'ai chi combines deep breathing and relaxation with slow and gentle movements. Originally developed in thirteenth-century China as a martial art, it is today practised around the world. Sometimes t'ai chi is referred to as 'meditation in motion'. The deliberate, controlled movements and intense concentration required help still the mind and give a deeper sense of relaxation to aid the release of inner tension and increase awareness.

IN ORDER TO EXPERIENCE
EVERYDAY SPIRITUALITY,
WE NEED TO REMEMBER
THAT WE ARE SPIRITUAL
BEINGS SPENDING SOME
TIME IN A HUMAN BODY.

Barbara de Angelis

Instead of dwelling on the past or worrying about the future, slow down and steady your thoughts. Start each day anew. The past has gone forever; the future hasn't yet arrived. Tap into your feelings as they unfold and search for the beauty in the now.

Create a peaceful space in your life when you can pray, meditate or perhaps practise yoga. A little quiet time and reflection at the end of each day can be beneficial in helping you to develop your spirituality.

OUR SPIRITUALITY
CREATES OUR WORLD
BECAUSE OUR LIVES
ARE A REFLECTION
OF WHATEVER WE
HOLD IN OUR MINDS.

David Lawrence Preston

AIKIDO

This Japanese martial art, 'the Art of Peace', promotes inner peace, unifies mind and body and encourages calm and relaxation. It aims to harmonise energy and movement in the act of self-defence: it requires little strength on the part of the practitioner and instead deflects the energy of the attacker as the means of defence. Its developer, O-Sensei, emphasised the moral and spiritual aspects of the art, particularly the development of harmony and peace.

Know that you are a spiritual being in a physical body, a soul with a body. Accepting this will change your attitude for the better towards many things in your life.

PHYSICAL STRENGTH CAN
NEVER PERMANENTLY
WITHSTAND THE IMPACT
OF SPIRITUAL FORCE.

Franklin D. Roosevelt

Do not hesitate if you are really determined to do something, even if others tell you that it will be impossible. Do not lose sight of the fact that we are all capable of doing much more than we think. Have faith in yourself.

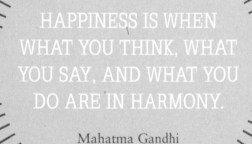

HAPPINESS IS WHEN
WHAT YOU THINK, WHAT
YOU SAY, AND WHAT YOU
DO ARE IN HARMONY.

Mahatma Gandhi

Do things you really enjoy doing. This helps free your mind of clutter, work and worry. Allowing yourself time to explore your passions opens up pathways to reach your inner spirit.

Make time to take several deep breaths at least once a day to bring a sense of peace to the body and mind.

STRETCHING

Stretching realigns the energy flow in your body. It is a universal method of gaining muscle movement and flexibility and is practised by both humans and animals, often almost sub-consciously, after periods of rest, sleep or inactivity. Start by concentrating on each part of your body, beginning with your toes. As you progress up your body, feel the wave of energy moving through a particular area and stretch all the respective muscles for a moment. Repeat this until you reach the top of your head, then give a full stretch, tensing all the muscles in your whole body and then relax completely.

SPIRITUALITY DOES TWO
THINGS FOR YOU. ONE, YOU
ARE FORCED TO BECOME
MORE SELFLESS, TWO, YOU
TRUST TO PROVIDENCE.

Imran Khan

Practise gratitude and you will find happiness. Ungrateful people cannot be truly happy.

Learn to live more spiritually by aiming to grow in openness, prudence and wisdom. These are key qualities possessed by many icons of spirituality.

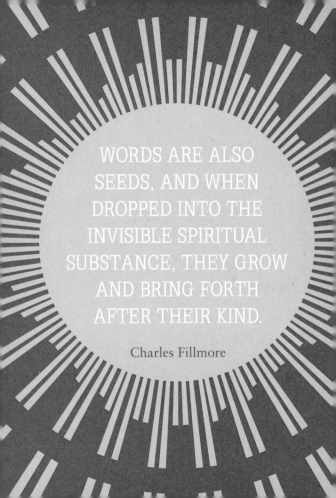

WORDS ARE ALSO
SEEDS, AND WHEN
DROPPED INTO THE
INVISIBLE SPIRITUAL
SUBSTANCE, THEY GROW
AND BRING FORTH
AFTER THEIR KIND.

Charles Fillmore

FASTING

Many religions and traditions practise some sort of fasting, which generally means going without food for a certain period of time in order to purify the body. Hippocrates recommended fasting; it is observed during the Islamic holy period of Ramadan, during Yom Kippur in Judaism, and the Catholic faith also observes this practice on Ash Wednesday and Good Friday. Fasting requires physical and psychological discipline and is seen by many as an inner journey to increase spiritual sensitivity.

There is a relationship between faith and a sense of purpose in life. A defined purpose gives our lives meaning and this in turn gives us a sense of well-being.

THE MEANING OF LIFE
IS TO FIND YOUR GIFT.
THE PURPOSE OF LIFE
IS TO GIVE IT AWAY.

Pablo Picasso

Whenever you are facing a difficult decision and have no idea what to do, take stock of the situation. You have all the answers deep inside you and will discover them by connecting with your inner feelings.

CHANGING THE WAY YOU
DO ROUTINE THINGS
ALLOWS A NEW PERSON
TO GROW INSIDE OF YOU.

Paulo Coelho

Make a conscious effort to act more impulsively. Free your mind and allow yourself to feel more carefree and laugh more – both at everyday situations and at yourself. Laughter can heal the soul.

'Healthy body, healthy mind' the saying goes, and this can extend to matters of the spirit. A properly nourished body is a sound ship which can be guided confidently and reliably by the mind, at the helm, through the waters of the soul.

SPIRITUAL HEALING

Try this ancient art for yourself by sitting quietly with your eyes closed. Imagine gold-coloured roots coming out of your body to ground you. Picture drawing up energy through your body and lighting up each of the chakras – the base of your spine, your groin, your solar plexus, your heart, your throat, your brow and your crown. See each one as a different coloured flame, each growing in intensity until it sets the next one alight. Finally, imagine the chakra in the top of your head opening to allow in universal energy with a brilliant white light. Take a few moments to surround yourself in that light.

WHEN YOU ARE KIND TO
OTHERS IT NOT ONLY
CHANGES YOU, IT ALSO
CHANGES THE WORLD.

Harold Kushner

What makes you feel grateful in your life? Take time to think about these things and write them down. Consider things that make you feel better, make you happy, that give you a warm feeling inside. Try to put a few minutes aside every day to do this. Gratitude makes you focus on life's positive aspects.

Dispel those feelings that you are unworthy, that you do not deserve wealth, happiness and joy. Do not think that others are better, more intelligent, more attractive than you are. We do not know the inner turmoil or challenges others may be facing in their personal lives. We find contentment when we find and follow our own path in life.

CRYSTAL THERAPY

Placed on or around the body, crystals
are used to magnify the effects of
hands-on healing. A therapist will
place crystals around the person being
treated, or on their chakras. Every
crystal contains the natural energy of
the earth and can enhance positivity.
The overall effect of this treatment is
to balance energies and help change
negative feelings into positive thoughts.
Healing crystals are also used for
divination and meditation purposes.

Remember, we can neither change what has gone before nor the way that other people act. What we can do is to keep a positive attitude and know there is a reason for everything.

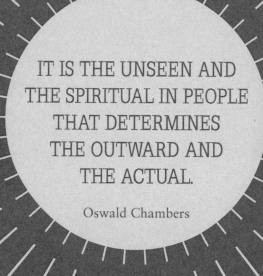

IT IS THE UNSEEN AND
THE SPIRITUAL IN PEOPLE
THAT DETERMINES
THE OUTWARD AND
THE ACTUAL.

Oswald Chambers

EACH DAY IS A DIFFERENT
ONE; EACH DAY BRINGS A
MIRACLE OF ITS OWN.

Paulo Coelho

There are no such things as mistakes. Regard everything as a lesson in becoming wiser at the art of living.

REIKI

The name of this type of ancient spiritual healing comprises two Japanese words meaning 'a higher power' and 'life force energy'. The reiki master acts as a channel to transmit healing energy to the person being treated by placing their hands over twelve different positions on the body, to encourage vital energy to flow. This helps to rebalance and increase the 'life force energy' which flows through us.

Trust in your spirituality to help you feel happier and less stressed. Spirituality is the part of your life that stays with you no matter what. With spirituality as your support, you can handle whatever life throws your way.

A SPIRITUAL
PARTNERSHIP IS
BETWEEN PEOPLE WHO
PROMISE THEMSELVES
TO USE ALL OF THEIR
EXPERIENCES TO
GROW SPIRITUALLY.

Gary Zukav

Let go of resentment, which holds you back and makes your thoughts heavy. Do not concern yourself or worry about what could have been. Concentrate on the present, because that is what matters.

When you feel things are difficult in your life, change the story in your head. Looking at things from a different perspective can help get you through bad times.

THE LAST AND GREATEST
OF HUMAN FREEDOMS IS
THE ABILITY TO CHOOSE
ONE'S ATTITUDE IN ANY
GIVEN CIRCUMSTANCE.

Viktor Frankl

SENSORY DEPRIVATION

This practice totally relaxes the mind and body. When suspended in a flotation tank of water heated to body temperature in a dark, silent room, sensual deprivation causes the brainwaves to switch to a state of meditation, bringing complete relaxation to the body. The water used contains a high concentration of salt, which aids buoyancy and means the skin does not wrinkle.

The past is behind us, the future is ahead of us. It is only ever the present that is always with us.

GRANT ME THE SERENITY
TO ACCEPT THE THINGS
I CANNOT CHANGE, THE
COURAGE TO CHANGE
THE THINGS I CAN AND
THE WISDOM TO KNOW
THE DIFFERENCE.

Reinhold Niebuhr

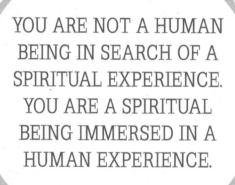

YOU ARE NOT A HUMAN
BEING IN SEARCH OF A
SPIRITUAL EXPERIENCE.
YOU ARE A SPIRITUAL
BEING IMMERSED IN A
HUMAN EXPERIENCE.

Pierre Teilhard de Chardin

From time to time, try to reduce the external noise all around you – television, radios and other appliances – to allow yourself peace of mind to connect with your inner thoughts.

Your inner potential has no limits. It is up to you to decide how much you want to make of it, about the direction you want your life to go. No one is holding you back from doing anything except yourself.

Take time to learn about other types of belief systems. Develop an open mind in order to discover ideas and points of view different from your own.

BAHÁ'Í

This relatively new religion was
established in Iran in 1863 by
Bahá'u'lláh. Followers believe in unity,
the equality of men and women and
working together for the common
good; that we are all part of the same
race and that the human soul does
not die. They believe God reveals
himself in stages and that the gods
of all other religions, which they
also accept and respect, are part of
this gradual revelation process, the
founder, Bahá'u'lláh, being the latest in
the line of revelations, but not the last.

MAKE FRIENDS WITH THE
ANGELS, WHO THOUGH
INVISIBLE ARE ALWAYS WITH
YOU. OFTEN INVOKE THEM,
CONSTANTLY PRAISE THEM,
AND MAKE GOOD USE OF
THEIR HELP AND ASSISTANCE
IN ALL YOUR TEMPORAL
AND SPIRITUAL AFFAIRS.

St Francis de Sales

Whatever you choose to think is up to you, but remember what the Roman, Marcus Aurelius wrote: 'A man's life is what his thoughts make of it.' It makes sense, then, to think only thoughts that content you.

Believe and trust that there is something positive to be found even during life's tough times and know that everything is happening as it should.

HAPPINESS IS NOT
SOMETHING READYMADE.
IT COMES FROM YOUR
OWN ACTIONS.

Dalai Lama

BUDDHISM

Buddhism is the pursuit of the spiritual
state of enlightenment through
practices like meditation, reflection
and rituals, including chanting. The
aim is to reach the transcendent
state of nirvana by following the
path of the Buddha, Siddhārtha
Gautama, who began his own quest
for enlightenment between the sixth
and fourth centuries BCE. Buddhists,
who do not worship gods, are known
for their peaceful demeanour, charity
and compassion towards others.

When we grow spiritually, we discard unrealistic concepts, thoughts and ideas. We learn to listen to our inner voice, to live in love, positivity and light and naturally become more conscious of and responsive to our inner being.

THOUSANDS OF CANDLES
CAN BE LIGHTED FROM A
SINGLE CANDLE, AND
THE LIFE OF THE CANDLE
WILL NOT BE SHORTENED.
HAPPINESS NEVER DECREASES
BY BEING SHARED.

Buddha

Do something for others without expecting anything back – simple things, like opening a door for someone, helping a colleague in the workplace, paying someone a compliment. There are no end of random acts of kindness you can do every day to bring you closer to a spiritual place.

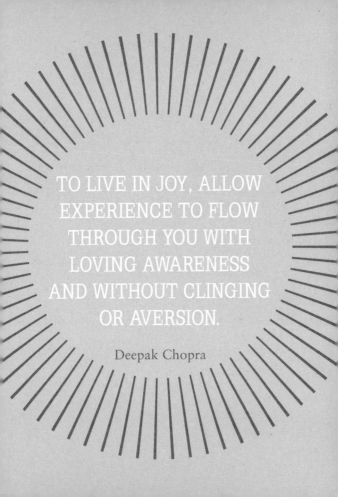

TO LIVE IN JOY, ALLOW
EXPERIENCE TO FLOW
THROUGH YOU WITH
LOVING AWARENESS
AND WITHOUT CLINGING
OR AVERSION.

Deepak Chopra

When unhappy thoughts come into your mind, do not dwell on them. Allow them to pass by and give yourself time to appreciate the positive aspects of each situation you experience. Always try to stay positive and believe that good things will happen.

What we give out to others, either in thought or deed, we get back. Remember that you are what you do, not what you say you will do.

KARMA

Karma is an invisible agent,
defined by the principle that every
action has a reaction; actions
have consequences. In effect,
this means what we give out, we
get back, not necessarily in this
world, but in future lives. It is
the law of cause and effect. The
law of karma says, 'When birds
are live, they eat ants. When the
birds die, ants eat the birds.'

Recall those times you have been upset because someone let you down. Maybe they didn't meet you at an arranged time or place or they didn't call you when they told you they would. Now consider the times that you have done the same to others and make a promise to yourself that this will not happen again.

EMPATHY IS REALLY THE OPPOSITE OF SPIRITUAL MEANNESS. IT'S THE CAPACITY TO UNDERSTAND THAT EVERY WAR IS BOTH WON AND LOST.

Barbara Kingsolver

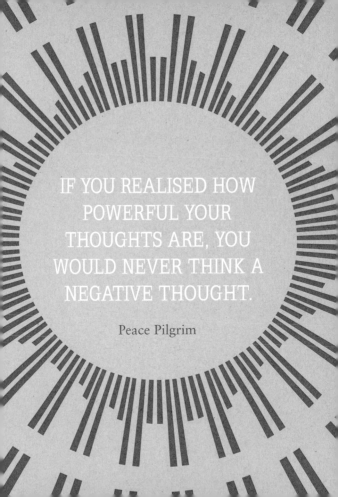

IF YOU REALISED HOW
POWERFUL YOUR
THOUGHTS ARE, YOU
WOULD NEVER THINK A
NEGATIVE THOUGHT.

Peace Pilgrim

When you understand that you attract the energy you give off, you realise that it makes a lot of sense to spread good vibrations, think positively and enjoy life.

HINDUISM

This is a collection of religious, philosophical and cultural ideas and practices characterised by the law of cause and effect, and following the path of righteousness. It has no single set of teachings, has its own beliefs, meaningful rituals and philosophy. Hinduism sees the soul as the essence of an individual – it is distinct from the body, senses and thoughts. Unlike the body, the soul is immortal and unchanging.

MY WISDOM FLOWS FROM
THE HIGHEST SOURCE. I
SALUTE THAT SOURCE IN
YOU. LET US WORK TOGETHER
FOR UNITY AND LOVE.

Mahatma Gandhi

THERE ARE NO ACCIDENTS...
THERE IS ONLY SOME
PURPOSE THAT WE HAVEN'T
YET UNDERSTOOD.

Deepak Chopra

Put your faith in the spiritual and allow yourself to release your old assumptions of how you feel your life should be. When you bring a more spiritual side into your life, you learn to trust that the universe, or the divine, has your best interests at heart.

When negative thoughts enter your mind, gently push them away. Remember, we have the power to control our thoughts and it is our choice whether we think positively or negatively.

THOUGH YOU MAY TRAVEL
THE WORLD TO FIND THE
BEAUTIFUL, YOU MUST
HAVE IT WITHIN YOU OR
YOU WILL FIND IT NOT.

Ralph Waldo Emerson

SIKHISM

Sikhism, based on the teachings of
Guru Nanak (1469–1539) and his nine
followers, teaches there is only one
god for all religions. The philosophy
is based more on the belief of doing
good works, treating everyone as
equals, meditation and always keeping
God in mind, rather than religious
ceremony. Sikhs' place of worship
is the gurdwara, where they learn
spiritual enlightenment and which may
also be used as a community centre.

Charitable endeavour, like faith, gives meaning to our lives and it is a truly reliable source of joy if we give it a try.

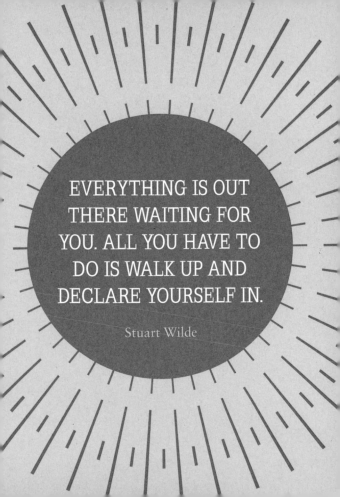

EVERYTHING IS OUT THERE WAITING FOR YOU. ALL YOU HAVE TO DO IS WALK UP AND DECLARE YOURSELF IN.

Stuart Wilde

There is always movement in life. When it is in chaos, find calm; when it is stagnant, move it along. Do not just sit and watch the world go by. You have the choice for change within you.

A random act of kindness is about doing something nice for someone who doesn't expect it. Try to make three people smile each day, perhaps by saying 'good morning' to a stranger, by giving a compliment or offering someone your seat on the train or bus.

HAPPINESS IS SPIRITUAL,
BORN OF TRUTH AND
LOVE. IT IS UNSELFISH;
THEREFORE IT CANNOT
EXIST ALONE, BUT REQUIRES
ALL MANKIND TO SHARE IT.

Mary Baker Eddy

SHAMANISM

Shamanism, an ancient form of
spiritual healing, is a journey into
'non-ordinary reality' through a
change in consciousness attained
through rhythmic drumming or
chanting. Shamans believe that the
root cause of all problems, whether
emotional or physical, is a spiritual
imbalance. They request healing and
advice from compassionate animals
and humans in the spirit world
and channel these transcendental
energies into this world.

Plant herbs in a pot in the house or in the garden. Fresh herbs bring you into direct contact with nature which, according to Native American healing methods, is the first step to finding physical and spiritual balance.

WE DO NOT NEED MORE
INTELLECTUAL POWER,
WE NEED MORE SPIRITUAL
POWER. WE DO NOT NEED
MORE OF THE THINGS
THAT ARE SEEN, WE NEED
MORE OF THE THINGS
THAT ARE UNSEEN.

Calvin Coolidge

EVERYTHING THAT
IRRITATES US ABOUT
OTHERS CAN LEAD US
TO AN UNDERSTANDING
OF OURSELVES.

Carl Jung

Plants, trees in particular, give off positive energy. Spend time in nature and you will feel uplifted. If you feel you need an extra boost of strength, being around oak trees will help. If you feel tense, willow trees will help calm you down.

Forgive. It is difficult – virtually impossible – to bring a more spiritual approach into your life when you feel angry, defensive, bitter or awash with resentment against another person. Always try to find the good in others.

You will not lose your way in life if you take time to listen to and trust in your enlightened inner voice.

CONFUCIANISM

The teachings of Chinese philosopher Confucius (551–479 BCE) derive from the idea that the everyday is sacred – that human beings are perfectible through self-cultivation and self-creation. To achieve this one has to uphold a number of ethical principles – honesty, modesty, forgiveness and, chiefly, humaneness. Though not overtly spiritual, in the respect of focussing on the elusive or ethereal, this practice supports the idea that ethical discipline engenders a stronger connection to the sacred.

Spirituality is a practice that can be learned, developed and applied. Learn more about how you can understand things and take time for reflection to tune into your inner self.

UNLESS WE ADVANCE
ENOUGH THROUGH
SPIRITUAL PRACTICES WE
WILL NOT BE ABLE TO FIND
PEACE IN THIS LIFETIME.

Yogi Cameron Alborzian

WE CANNOT DO GREAT
THINGS ON THIS EARTH,
ONLY SMALL THINGS
WITH GREAT LOVE.

Mother Teresa

When we were children we were told 'it is better to give than to receive'. Perhaps then we did not believe it, but it is indeed true. The gratification experienced after doing something for others brings a sense of contentment. Selfish pleasures do not provide meaning to our lives. Spreading good helps make the world a better and brighter place.

Take time to observe the beauty of nature. The form and function of a bird are in complete harmony; there is poetry in its flight, yet this is simply how it moves from A to B. Consider the harmony of your own thoughts and actions as you go about your daily business.

SHINTO

Shinto has no founder, no single god nor a set of rules. Followers believe in spirits called *kami*, which exist in all objects. They also believe that they should exist in harmony with nature, as well as with other religions. Their belief is that human beings are basically good, and that evil is the result of invading spirits. Whilst shinto often focuses on local devotion at many shrines, it is also seen as the indigenous religion of Japan.

REMEMBER HAPPINESS
DOESN'T DEPEND UPON
WHO YOU ARE OR WHAT YOU
HAVE; IT DEPENDS SOLELY
ON WHAT YOU THINK.

Dale Carnegie

Count your blessings. Acknowledging those blessings that we have in our lives helps bring in more positivity.

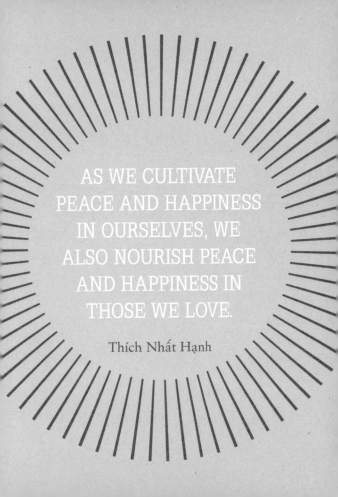

AS WE CULTIVATE
PEACE AND HAPPINESS
IN OURSELVES, WE
ALSO NOURISH PEACE
AND HAPPINESS IN
THOSE WE LOVE.

Thích Nhất Hạnh

Open your eyes and heart to find the daily blessings in your life and when you do, be sure to treasure them.

JAINISM

This ancient Indian belief dates back to the sixth century BCE. Followers believe all living things have souls of equal value and that liberation is achieved in practising non-violence and vegetarianism. There are no gods in Jainism, but there is a belief in reincarnation and karma, and that the goal of spiritual life is release from the birth–death cycle.

When you have a quiet moment in your day, use the time to think positively about yourself and those around you. By doing so, you will help strengthen your power of thought and improve your concentration.

To live spiritually depends on our thoughts, emotions, beliefs and desires. When we find a spiritual dimension it means we have succeeded in finding a way to achieve inner peace and true contentment as we follow life's path.

A MAN IS BUT THE PRODUCT
OF HIS THOUGHTS. WHAT
HE THINKS, HE BECOMES.

Mahatma Gandhi

Happiness is what comes to us when we live our lives with grace and gratitude. Before you can truly love others, you need to learn to love yourself. To find happiness, let go of negative beliefs, emotions and things which are holding you back in life.

Many of us multi-task in these hectic times, but doing so actually makes us less productive. While at first it may feel extremely strange, turning off the phone or computer for even an hour is the first step to focus on and connect with yourself and your spirituality.

START BY DOING WHAT'S NECESSARY, THEN DO WHAT'S POSSIBLE; AND SUDDENLY YOU ARE DOING THE IMPOSSIBLE.

St Francis of Assisi

If you believe good things will come to you, they will. The best things come to those who don't give up.

Focus your mind, take a step back from the here and now. Only by standing back can you see things as they really are.

THEOSOPHY

Meaning 'wisdom of the gods', theosophy refers to hidden knowledge or mystical insight that offers enlightenment and salvation. Theosophists access spiritual reality through mystical experience, support concepts such as reincarnation and karma, and follow practices including vegetarianism and meditation. The theosophist seeks to understand the mysteries of the universe and the bonds that unite humanity and the divine.

BY HAVING A REVERENCE
FOR LIFE, WE ENTER INTO
A SPIRITUAL RELATION
WITH THE WORLD.

Albert Schweitzer

When we start to live spiritually we allow our inner values to guide how we interact with the world around us. Bringing spirituality into our own world gives us more self-knowledge and self-empowerment and above all, more peace in our day-to-day lives.

The freedom of choice is yours, wherever you are, whatever you do. Whether you choose to be happy or sad, friendly or unsociable, trustworthy or unreliable, it's your call.

The spiritual journey is an intensely personal one. Look within yourself to discover what it really is that you want from your life. Ask yourself what your life purpose is.

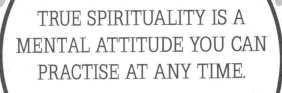

TRUE SPIRITUALITY IS A
MENTAL ATTITUDE YOU CAN
PRACTISE AT ANY TIME.

Dalai Lama

FURTHER READING

Barry, Dylan *Zen Buddhism: Understanding the Buddha's Teachings of Zen* (2014, Happy Dhamma)

Brady, Peter *Aikido Step by Step* (2013, Lorenz Books)

Dhilon, Harish *The First Sikh Spiritual Master: Timeless Wisdom from the Life and Teachings of Guru Nanak* (2006, Skylight Paths Publishing)

Elliott Price, Sara *Meditation for Beginners: How to Meditate For Lifelong Peace, Focus and Happiness* (2014, Amazon Media EU)

Isaacs, Nora *The Little Book of Yoga* (2014, Chronicle Books)

Jaini, Jagmanderlal *Outlines of Jainism* (reprint 2013, Cambridge University Press)

Liu, Dr Tiamjun *The Key to the Qigong Meditation State: The Art and Science of Chinese Energy Healing* by (2014, Singing Dragon)

Meredith, Scott and Ray, Jeremy *Tai Chi Peng Root Power Rising* by (2014, Create Space)

Preston, David Lawrence *365 Steps to Practical Spirituality* (2007, How To Books)

Wilkinson, Tony *The Lost Art of Being Happy* (2007, Findhorn Press Ltd)

THE GIFT OF
MINDFULNESS

YVETTE JANE

THE GIFT OF
HAPPINESS

YVETTE JANE

THE GIFT OF
HEALING

YVETTE JANE

THE GIFT OF MINDFULNESS
(978 1 84953 605 9)

THE GIFT OF HAPPINESS
(978 1 84953 606 6)

THE GIFT OF HEALING
(978 1 84953 607 3)

Yvette Jane

Hardback   £5.99

'THE PURPOSE OF OUR
LIVES IS TO BE HAPPY.'

Dalai Lama

These books of uplifting wisdom and
inspiring quotations will help you ease
into a thankful and joyful state of mind,
allowing you to meet each day with a
renewed sense of gladness.

If you're interested in finding out more about our books, find us on Facebook at **Summersdale Publishers** and follow us on Twitter at **@Summersdale**.

BREAKFAST MARTINI

1¾ measures gin

½ measure Cointreau

¾ measure lemon juice

1 tsp orange marmalade

orange and a small slice of toast, to garnish

Add all the ingredients to a cocktail shaker and give
the liquid a quick stir to break up the marmalade.

Shake vigorously with cubed ice and double strain into
a chilled martini glass.

Garnish with an orange twist and a small slice of toast.

SOUTHSIDE

2 measures gin

4 teaspoons lime juice

4 teaspoons sugar syrup

5 mint leaves plus extra, to garnish

Add all the ingredients to a cocktail shaker with some ice cubes.

Shake and strain into a martini glass.

Garnish with a mint leaf and serve.

GIBSON
MARTINI

2½ measures gin

½ measure dry vermouth

cocktail onions, to garnish

Add the gin and dry vermouth to a cocktail shaker,
and fill with cubed ice.

Stir for 30 seconds, and strain into a chilled martini glass.

Garnish generously with cocktail onions.

DOOBS
MARTINI

1¾ measures gin

1 measure sloe gin

¾ measure dry vermouth

4 dashes orange bitters

orange, to garnish

Add all the ingredients to a cocktail shaker and fill
with cubed ice.

Stir for 30 seconds, and strain into a chilled martini glass.

Garnish with an orange twist.

CLASSIC
MARTINI

makes 2

1 measure dry vermouth

6 measures gin

stuffed green olives, to garnish

Put 10–12 ice cubes into a mixing glass.

Pour over the vermouth and gin, then stir (never shake) vigorously and evenly, without splashing.

Strain into 2 chilled martini glasses, garnish each with a green olive and serve.

HANKY
PANKY

2 measures gin

1 measure sweet vermouth

1 tablespoon Fernet Branca

orange, to garnish

Add all the ingredients to a cocktail shaker and fill
with cubed ice.

Stir for 30 seconds, and strain into a chilled martini glass.

Garnish with an orange twist.

VESPER
MARTINI

2½ measures gin

1 measure vodka

½ measure Lillet Blanc

lemon, to garnish

Add all the ingredients to a cocktail shaker and fill the top half of it with ice.

Shake vigorously and double strain into a chilled martini glass.

Garnish with a lemon twist.

GIN GARDEN
MARTINI

makes 2

4 measures gin

2 measures pressed apple juice

1 measure elderflower cordial

½ cucumber, peeled and chopped, plus extra slices,
to garnish

Muddle the cucumber in the bottom of a
cocktail shaker with the elderflower cordial.

Add the gin, apple juice and some ice cubes.

Shake and double-strain into 2 chilled martini glasses,
garnish with peeled cucumber slices and serve.

ESPRESSO GIN-TINI

1½ measures gin

1 measure coffee liqueur

1 measure fresh espresso coffee

½ measure sugar syrup

3 coffee beans, to garnish

Add all the ingredients to a cocktail shaker.

Shake vigorously and double strain into a chilled martini glass.

Garnish with the 3 coffee beans.

LYCHEE
MARTINI

1½ measures gin

1 measure lychee liqueur

½ measure lychee syrup (from the tin)

¾ measure lemon juice

lychees (tinned), to garnish

Add all the ingredients to a cocktail shaker, shake vigorously and double strain into a chilled martini glass.

Garnish with lychees.

RED
RUM

makes 2

1 measure sloe gin

handful of redcurrants plus extra, to garnish

4 measures Bacardi 8-year-old rum

1 measure lemon juice

1 measure vanilla syrup

Muddle the sloe gin and redcurrants together
in a cocktail shaker.

Add the rum, lemon juice, vanilla syrup and some
ice cubes.

Shake and double-strain into 2 chilled martini
glasses, garnish with redcurrants and serve.

FLUTES &
COUPETTES

ARMY & NAVY

2 measures gin

1 measure lemon juice

½ measure orgeat syrup

lemon, to garnish

Add all the ingredients to a cocktail shaker.

Shake vigorously with cubed ice and double strain into
a chilled coupette glass.

Garnish with a lemon twist.

BEES KNEES

2 measures gin

1 measure lemon juice

½ measure honey

lemon, to garnish

Add all the ingredients to a cocktail shaker.

Shake vigorously with cubed ice, double strain into a chilled coupette glass and garnish with a lemon twist.

CLOVER CLUB

2 measures gin

¾ measure lemon juice

¾ measure sugar syrup

5 raspberries

½ measure egg white

Add all the ingredients to a cocktail shaker and vigorously dry-shake without ice for 10 seconds.

Take the shaker apart, add cubed ice and shake again vigorously.

Strain into a coupette glass and garnish with raspberries.

FRENCH 75

makes 2

2 measures gin

6 teaspoons lemon juice

6 teaspoons sugar syrup

8 measures Champagne

lemon twist, to garnish

Add the gin, lemon juice and sugar syrup
into a cocktail shaker and shake.

Strain into 2 flute glasses and top with the
chilled Champagne.

Garnish with a lemon twist and serve.

GIMLET

2½ measures gin

½ measure lime cordial

½ measure lime juice

lime, to garnish

Add all the ingredients to a cocktail shaker, shake vigorously and strain into a chilled coupette glass.

Garnish with a lime twist.

PERFECT
LADY

1½ measures gin

¾ measure lemon juice

½ measure peach liqueur

½ measure egg white

Add all the ingredients to a cocktail shaker and
vigorously dry-shake without ice for 10 seconds.

Take the shaker apart, add cubed ice and shake vigorously.

Double strain into a chilled coupette glass.

No garnish.

FRENCH
PINK LADY

2 measures gin

1 measure triple sec

4 raspberries

3 teaspoons lime juice

1 teaspoon pastis

lime wedge, to garnish

Add all the ingredients except for the lime wedge
to a cocktail shaker and muddle.

Fill the shaker with ice cubes and shake, then strain into
a coupette glass.

Garnish with a lime wedge and serve.

WHITE LADY

1½ measures gin

1 measure Cointreau

¾ measure lemon juice

lemon, to garnish

Add all the ingredients to a cocktail shaker, shake vigorously and double strain into a chilled coupette glass.

Garnish with a lemon twist.

SATAN'S
WHISKERS

1½ measures gin

½ measure orange curaçao

½ measure sweet vermouth

½ measure dry vermouth

1½ measures orange juice

2 dashes orange bitters

Add all the ingredients to a cocktail shaker, shake
vigorously and double strain into a chilled coupette glass.

No garnish.

MARTINEZ

2 measures gin

1 measure sweet vermouth

1 teaspoon Maraschino

2 dashes Angostura bitters

orange twist, to garnish

Add all the ingredients to a cocktail
shaker and fill with cubed ice.

Stir for 30 seconds and strain into a chilled coupette glass.

Garnish with an orange twist.

CORPSE
REVIVER NO. 2

1 measure gin

1 measure lemon juice

1 measure Lillet Blanc

1 measure Cointreau

2 drops absinthe

lemon, to garnish

Add all the ingredients to a cocktail shaker.

Shake vigorously with cubed ice and double strain into a chilled coupette glass.

Garnish with a lemon twist.

LONDON CALLING

1½ measures gin

¾ measure lemon juice

¾ measure Fino sherry

½ measure sugar syrup

2 dashes Angostura bitters

lemon, to garnish

Add all the ingredients to a cocktail shaker, shake vigorously and strain into a chilled coupette glass.

Garnish with a lemon twist.

ROYAL
COBBLER

3 teaspoons gin

3 teaspoons Fino sherry

3 teaspoons raspberry and pineapple syrup

2 teaspoons lemon juice

3 measures Prosecco

raspberry, to garnish

Add the gin, Fino sherry, raspberry and pineapple
syrup and lemon juice to a cocktail shaker.

Shake and strain into a flute glass and top with
chilled Prosecco.

Garnish with a raspberry or orange twist and serve.

GOLDEN
DAWN

1 measure gin

1 measure Calvados

1 measure apricot brandy

1½ measures orange juice

2 teaspoons grenadine

2 dashes Angostura bitters

lemon, to garnish

Add all the ingredients except the grenadine to a cocktail shaker, shake vigorously and strain into a coupette glass.

Carefully add the grenadine, allowing it to float to the bottom of the glass to create a "sunrise" effect.

Garnish with a lemon twist.

LADY OF
LEISURE

1 measure gin

½ measure Chambord

½ measure Cointreau

¼ measure lemon juice

1 measure pineapple juice

orange, to garnish

Add all the ingredients to a cocktail shaker, shake
vigorously and strain into a coupette glass.

Garnish with an orange twist.

ROCKS & WINE GLASSES

BRAMBLE

2 measures gin

1 measure lemon juice

½ measure sugar syrup

½ measure crème de mûre

lemon and blackberries, to garnish

Fill a rocks glass with crushed ice, packing it in tightly.

Add the gin, lemon juice and sugar syrup and stir briefly.

Slowly drizzle over the crème de mûre, so that it creates
a "bleeding" effect down through the drink.

Top with more crushed ice and garnish with
blackberries and a lemon wedge.

NEGRONI

1 measure gin

1 measure sweet vermouth

1 measure Campari

orange wedges, to garnish

Add all the ingredients to a rocks glass
filled with ice cubes and stir.

Garnish with an orange twist and serve.

LYCHEE
NEGRONI

¾ measure gin

1½ measures bianco vermouth

½ measure Campari

1 measure lychee juice

cucumber, to garnish

Add all the ingredients to a rocks glass full of cubed ice, stir briefly and garnish with a slice of cucumber.

GIN
RICKEY

2 measures gin

¾ measure lime juice

½ measure sugar syrup

soda water, to top

lime, to garnish

Add all the ingredients to a large wine glass
full of cubed ice, stir briefly and garnish with
a lemon wedge and a sprig of mint.

GINNY
GIN FIZZ

2 measures gin

1 camomile tea bag

1 measure sugar syrup

1 measure lemon juice

3 teaspoons egg white

3 measures soda water

lemon twist, to garnish

Place the gin and camomile tea bag in a cocktail
shaker and leave to infuse for 2 minutes.

Remove the tea bag, add the sugar syrup,
lemon juice and egg white.

Fill the shaker with ice cubes.

Shake and strain into a wine glass filled with
ice cubes and top with the soda water.

Garnish with a lemon twist and serve.

GIN
CUP

2 measures gin

¾ measure lemon juice

½ measure sugar syrup

3 mint sprigs, plus extra to garnish

Muddle the mint and sugar syrup in a rocks glass.

Fill the glass with crushed ice, add the gin and lemon and churn vigorously until a frost begins to form on the glass.

Garnish with mint sprigs.

SLOE GIN
SOUR

2 measures sloe gin

1 measure lemon juice

1 measure sugar syrup

½ measure egg white

2 dashes Peychaud's bitters

orange, to garnish

Add all the ingredients to a cocktail shaker and dry-shake without ice for 10 seconds, take the shaker apart and add cubed ice.

Shake vigorously and double strain into an old fashioned glass filled with cubed ice.

Garnish with an orange slice.

ORANGE
BLOSSOM

2 measures gin

2 measures pink grapefruit juice

2 teaspoons orgeat

2 dashes Angostura bitters

4 orange slices

orange, to garnish

Muddle the orange slices and orgeat in a rocks glass, add
the remaining ingredients, fill with crushed ice and churn.

Top with more crushed ice and garnish with
orange wedges.

P&T

1½ measures pink gin

½ measure strawberry liqueur

½ measure lemon juice

equal parts tonic and soda water, to top

rosemary and grapefruit, to garnish

Add all the ingredients to a large wine glass
full of cubed ice, stir briefly and garnish with a
sprig of rosemary and a slice of grapefruit.

STRAWBERRY
FIELDS

2 measures gin

1 camomile tea bag

1 measure strawberry purée

2 teaspoons lemon juice

1 measure double cream

soda water, to top

strawberry, to garnish

Add the gin and tea bag to a cocktail shaker and leave to infuse for 2 minutes, stirring occasionally.

Remove the tea bag and add the rest of the ingredients to the shaker.

Shake vigorously, strain into a wine glass full of cubed ice, top with soda water and garnish with a strawberry.

GIN CUCUMBER
COOLER

2 measures gin

5 mint leaves

5 slices cucumber

3 measures apple juice

3 measures soda water

mint sprig, to garnish

Add the gin, mint and cucumber to
a rocks glass and gently muddle.

Leave to stand for a couple of minutes, then add
the apple juice, soda water and some ice cubes.

Garnish with a mint sprig.

HIGHBALLS

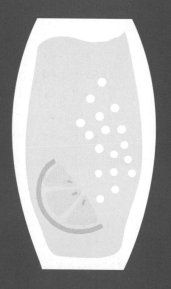

SAKE
COLLINS

1 measure gin

2 measures sake

½ measure lemon juice

¾ measure sugar syrup

½ measure grapefruit juice

soda water, to top

cucumber and grapefruit, to garnish

Add all the ingredients except the soda
water to a cocktail shaker.

Shake vigorously, strain into a highball glass
full of cubed ice and top with soda.

Garnish with a slice of grapefruit and a cucumber ribbon.

TOM COLLINS

2 measures gin

1 measure sugar syrup

1 measure lemon juice

4 measures soda water

lemon wedge, to garnish

Put the gin, sugar syrup and lemon juice into a cocktail shaker and fill with ice cubes.

Shake and strain into a highball glass full of ice cubes and top with the soda water.

Garnish with a lemon wedge.

HEDGEROW
COLLINS

1½ measures gin

½ measure crème de mûre

1 teaspoon Campari

¾ measure lemon juice

½ measure sugar syrup

soda water, to top

lemon and blackberry, to garnish

Add all the ingredients except the soda water
to a highball glass filled with cubed ice.

Stir gently, top with soda and garnish with
a lemon wedge and a blackberry.

BERRY
COLLINS

makes 2

8 raspberries plus extra,
to garnish

8 blueberries plus extra,
to garnish

1–2 dashes strawberry
syrup

4 measures gin

4 teaspoons lemon juice

sugar syrup, to taste

soda water, to top up

lemon slices, to garnish

Muddle the berries and strawberry syrup in the bottom of
two highball glasses, then fill each glass with crushed ice.

Add the gin, lemon juice and sugar syrup.

Stir, then top with the soda water.

Garnish with berries and lemon slices and serve.

CAMOMILE
COLLINS

2 measures gin

1 camomile tea bag

1 measure lemon juice

1 measure sugar syrup

4 measures soda water

lemon slice, to garnish

Pour the gin into a highball glass and add the tea bag.

Stir the tea bag and gin together, for about 5 minutes, until the gin is infused with the camomile flavour.

Remove the tea bag and fill the glass with ice cubes.

Add the remaining ingredients and garnish with a lemon slice.

BRITISH
MOJITO

2 measures gin

¾ measure lime juice

½ measure elderflower cordial

6–8 mint leaves

soda, to top

lime and mint, to garnish

Add all the ingredients except the soda water to
a highball glass.

Fill the glass with crushed ice, and churn with a bar spoon.

Add a splash of soda water, and top with more
crushed ice.

Garnish with a lime wedge and a mint sprig.

ELDERFLOWER
MOJITO

1½ measures gin

1 measure elderflower liqueur

½ measure lemon juice

equal parts tonic and soda water, to top

cucumber and mint, to garnish

Add all the ingredients to a highball
full of crushed ice and churn.

Top with more crushed ice and tonic as needed and
garnish with a cucumber slice and a sprig of mint.

PIMM'S
COCKTAIL

makes 2

2 measures Pimm's
No. 1 Cup

2 measures gin

4 measures lemonade

4 measures ginger ale

to garnish:

cucumber strips

blueberries

orange slices

Fill 2 highball glasses with ice cubes.

Add all the ingredients, one by one in order, over the ice.

Garnish with cucumber strips, blueberries
and orange slices and serve.

SINGAPORE
SLING

1 measure gin

1 measure Cointreau

½ measure Bénédictine

½ measure cherry brandy

¾ measure lemon juice

soda water, to top

lemon and cocktail cherry, to garnish

Add all the ingredients except the soda
water to a cocktail shaker.

Shake vigorously, strain into a hurricane glass
filled with cubed ice and top with soda water.

Garnish with a lemon wedge and cocktail cherry.

GIN &
IT

1½ measures gin

1½ measures sweet vermouth

orange, to garnish

Add all the ingredients to a rocks glass filled with cubed
ice, stir briefly and garnish with a slice of orange.

MANGO
RICKY

5 basil leaves plus extra, to garnish

2 lime wedges

1 measure mango-infused gin

2 teaspoons sugar syrup

2 measures soda water

Roughly tear the basil leaves and add to a highball glass.

Squeeze the lime wedges into the glass
and then add them to the glass.

Add the gin, sugar syrup and soda water,
then top the glass with crushed ice.

Garnish with basil leaves and serve.

FIX

2 measures gin

1 measure lemon juice

¾ measure sugar syrup

seasonal fruit, to garnish

Add all the ingredients to a rocks glass filled with crushed ice.

Churn, and garnish with seasonal fruit of your choosing.

G & TEA

1½ measures gin

¾ measure peach liqueur

¾ measure lemon juice

½ measure sugar syrup

2 measures cold breakfast tea

lemon and rosemary, to garnish

Add all the ingredients to a cocktail shaker,
shake vigorously and strain into a chilled
highball glass filled with cubed ice.

Garnish with a lemon wedge and a sprig of rosemary.

CHERRY
JULEP

¾ measure gin

¾ measure sloe gin

¾ measure cherry brandy

¾ measure lemon juice

1 teaspoon sugar syrup

1 teaspoon grenadine

lemon and mint, to garnish

Add all the ingredients to a highball glass filled
with crushed ice, and churn vigorously.

Top with more crushed ice and garnish with
a wedge of lemon and a mint sprig.

LONG ISLAND
ICED TEA

makes 2

1 measure vodka

1 measure gin

1 measure white rum

1 measure tequila

1 measure Cointreau

1 measure lemon juice

cola, to top up

lemon slices, to garnish

Put the vodka, gin, rum, tequila, Cointreau and lemon
juice in a cocktail shaker with some ice cubes and
shake to mix.

Strain into 2 highball glasses filled with
ice cubes and top with cola.

Garnish with lemon slices.

JUGS & BOWLS

MULLED GIN

6 measures apple juice

2 measures gin

1 cinnamon stick

2 star anise

4 whole cloves

1 dash lime juice

Add all the ingredients to a saucepan.

Heat the liquid gently (don't let it boil) to steep the spices.

After 10 minutes serve in heatproof glasses or mugs.

TWISTED
SANGRIA

4 measures gin

6 measures apple juice

2 measures lemon juice

2 measures elderflower cordial

6 measures white wine

6 measures soda water

apple, lemon and mint, to garnish

Add all the ingredients to a jug filled
with ice cubes and stir.

Garnish with apple and lemon slices and mint leaves.

LANGRA
AND TONIC

makes 1 large jug

200 ml (7 fl oz) gin

4 measures mango juice

2 measures lemon juice

2 measures sugar

200 ml (7 fl oz) tonic water

lemon wheels, to garnish

Add all the ingredients to a jug filled
with ice cubes and stir.

Garnish with lemon wheels and serve.

GARDEN
COOLER

makes 1 large punch bowl

700 ml (23½ fl oz)
London dry gin

500 ml (17 fl oz)
lemon juice

250 ml (8 fl oz) sugar syrup

250 ml (8 fl oz)
elderflower cordial

500 ml (17 fl oz) apple juice

500 ml (17 fl oz) green
tea, cooled

500 ml (17 fl oz)
mint tea, cooled

500 ml (17 fl oz)
soda water

peach slices,
to garnish

Add all the ingredients to a punch bowl
filled with ice cubes and stir.

Garnish with peach slices and serve.

EARL'S
PUNCH

makes 1 large jug

4 measures gin

6 measures Earl Grey
tea, chilled

6 measures pink
grapefruit juice

6 measures soda water

1 measure sugar syrup

to garnish:
pink grapefruit slices
black cherries

Add all the ingredients to a jug filled
with ice cubes and stir.

Garnish with pink grapefruit slices and black cherries
and serve.

BAR BASICS & TECHNIQUES

THE BASICS

Good cocktails, like good food, are based around quality ingredients. As with cooking, using fresh and homemade ingredients can often make the huge difference between a good drink and an outstanding drink. All of this can be found in department stores, online or in kitchen shops.

Ice

This is a key part of cocktails and you'll need lots of it. Purchase it from your supermarket, or freeze big tubs of water then crack them up to use in your drinks. If you're hosting a big party and want to serve some punches, which will need lots of ice, it may be worthwhile to find out if you have a local ice supplier that supplies catering companies, as this can be much more cost-effective.

Citrus juice

It's important to use fresh citrus juice; bottled versions taste awful and will not produce good drinks.

Store your fruit at room temperature. Look for a soft-skinned fruit for juicing, which you can do with a juicer or citrus press. You can keep fresh citrus juice for a couple of days in the refrigerator, sealed to prevent oxidation.

Sugar syrup

You can buy sugar syrup or you can make your own. The most basic form of sugar syrup is made by mixing caster sugar and hot water together, and stirring until the sugar has dissolved. The key is to use a 1:1 ratio of sugar to liquid. White sugar acts as a flavour enhancer, while dark sugars have unique, more toffee-like flavours that work well with dark spirits.

BASIC SUGAR SYRUP RECIPE

Makes 1 litre (1¾ pints)

1 kg (2 lb) caster sugar
1 litre (1¾ pints) hot water

Dissolve the caster sugar in the hot water.

Allow to cool.

The sugar syrup will keep in a sterilized bottle stored in the refrigerator for up to two weeks.

CHOOSING GLASSWARE

There are many different cocktails, but they all fall into one of three categories: long, short or shot. Long drinks generally have more mixer than alcohol, often served with ice and a straw. The terms "straight up" and "on the rocks" are synonymous with the short drink, which tends to be more about the spirit, often combined with a single mixer at most. Finally, there is the shot which is made up mainly from spirits and liqueurs, designed to give a quick hit of alcohol. Glasses are tailored to the type of drinks they will contain, each of which is described opposite.

Champagne flute

Used for Champagne or Champagne cocktails, the narrow mouth of the flute helps the drink to stay fizzy.

Champagne saucer

A classic glass, but not very practical for serving Champagne as the drink quickly loses its fizz.

Margarita or Coupette glass

When used for a Margarita, the rim is dipped in salt. Also used for daiquiris and other fruit-based cocktails.

Highball glass

Suitable for any long cocktail, such as a Long Island Iced Tea.

Collins glass

This is similar to a highball glass but is slightly narrower.

Wine glass

Sangria is often served in one, but they are not usually used for cocktails.

Old-Fashioned glass

Also known as a rocks glass, this is great for any drink that's served on the rocks or straight up.

Shot glass

Often found in two sizes – for a single or double measure. They are ideal for a single mouthful.

Balloon glass

Often used for fine spirits. The glass can be warmed to encourage the release of the drink's aroma.

Hurricane glass

Mostly found in beach bars, used for creamy, rum-based drinks.

Boston glass

Often used by bartenders for mixing fruity drinks.

Toddy glass

A toddy glass is generally used for a hot drink, such as Irish Coffee.

Sling glass

This has a very short stemmed base and is most famously used for a Singapore Sling.

Martini glass

Also known as a cocktail glass, its thin-neck design makes sure your hand can't warm the glass or the cocktail.

USEFUL EQUIPMENT

Some pieces of equipment, such as shakers and the correct glasses, are vital for any cocktail enthusiast. Below is a wish list of things to have to hand for anyone who wants to regularly make decent cocktails.

Shaker

The Boston shaker is the most simple option, but it needs to be used in conjunction with a hawthorne strainer. Alternatively you could choose a shaker with a built-in strainer.

Measure or jigger

Single and double measures are available and are essential when you are mixing ingredients so that the proportions are always the same. One measure is 25 ml or 1 fl oz.

Mixing glass

A mixing glass is used for those drinks that require only a gentle stirring before they are poured or strained.

Hawthorne strainer

This type of strainer is often used in conjunction with a Boston shaker, but a simple tea strainer will also work well.

Bar spoon

Similar to a teaspoon but with a long handle, a bar spoon is used for stirring, layering and muddling drinks.

Muddling stick

Similar to a pestle, which will work just as well, a muddling stick, or muddler, is used to crush fruit or herbs in a glass or shaker for drinks like the Mojito.

Bottle opener

Choose a bottle opener with two attachments, one for metal-topped bottles and a corkscrew for wine bottles.

Pourers

A pourer is inserted into the top of a spirit bottle to enable the spirit to flow in a controlled manner.

Food processor

A food processor or blender is useful for making frozen cocktails and smoothies.

Equipment for garnishing

Exotic drinks may be prettified with a paper umbrella and several long drinks are served with straws or swizzle sticks.

TECHNIQUES

With just a few basic techniques, your bartending skills will be complete. Follow the instructions to hone your craft.

Blending

Frozen cocktails and smoothies are blended with ice in a blender until they are of a smooth consistency. Be careful not to add too much ice as this will dilute the cocktail. It's best to add a little at a time.

Muddling

A technique used to bring out the flavours of herbs and fruit using a blunt tool called a muddler.

1. *Add chosen herb(s) to a highball glass. Add some sugar syrup and some lime wedges.*

2. *Hold the glass firmly and use a muddler or pestle to twist and press down.*

3. *Continue for 30 seconds, top with crushed ice and add the remaining ingredients.*

Shaking

The best-known cocktail technique and probably the most common. Used to mix ingredients thoroughly and quickly, and to chill the drink before serving.

1. *Half-fill a cocktail shaker with ice cubes, or cracked or crushed ice.*

2. *If the recipe calls for a chilled glass add a few ice cubes and some cold water to the glass, swirl it around and discard.*

3. *Add the ingredients to the shaker and shake until a frost forms on the outside.*

4. *Strain the cocktail into the glass and serve.*

Double-straining

To prevent all traces of puréed fruit and ice fragments from entering the glass, use a shaker with a built-in strainer in conjunction with a hawthorne strainer. A fine strainer also works well.

Layering

Some spirits can be served layered on top of each other, causing lighter spirits to float on top of your cocktail.

1. *Pour the first ingredient into a glass, taking care that it does not touch the sides.*

2. *Position a bar spoon in the centre of the glass, rounded part down and facing you. Rest the spoon against the side of the glass as your pour the second ingredient down the spoon. It should float on top of the first liquid.*

3. *Repeat with the third ingredient, then carefully remove the spoon.*

Stirring

Used when the ingredients need to be mixed and chilled, but also maintain their clarity. This ensures there are no ice fragments or air bubbles throughout the drink. Some cocktails require the ingredients to be prepared in a mixing glass, then strained into the serving glass.

1. *Add the ingredients to a glass, in recipe order.*

2. *Use a bar spoon to stir the drink, lightly or vigorously, as described in the recipe.*

3. *Finish the drink with any decoration and serve.*

INDEX

All photos © Octopus Publishing Group. Jonathan Kennedy 9, 27, 30, 37, 38, 45, 48, 56, 61, 64, 72, 81, 82, 85, 86; Stephen Conroy 12, 17, 20, 53, 69